Cool STEAM Careers

Sports Medicine Doctor

Samantha Bell

Published in the United States of America by Cherry Lake Publishing
Ann Arbor, Michigan
www.cherrylakepublishing.com

Content Adviser: Lauren E. Groves M.S. PA-C
Reading Adviser: Marla Conn, ReadAbility, Inc.

Photo Credits: © CEFutcher/iStock Images, cover, 1, 9, 12; © Nebojsa Markovic/Shutterstock.com, 5; © asiseeit/iStock Images, 6; © Creatas/Thinkstock Images, 10; © Monkey Business Images/Shutterstock Images, 15; © Kzenon/Shutterstock Images, 16; © dboystudio/Shutterstock.com, 17; © piotrwzk/Shutterstock Images, 18; © Natursports|Dreamstime.com-Injured Football Player Photo, 21; © Mitch Gunn/Shutterstock.com, 22; © Aspenphoto|Dreamstime.com-Girls High School Basketball Photo, 25; © Andresr/Shutterstock Images, 26; © Syda Productions/Shutterstock Images, 29

Library of Congress Cataloging-in-Publication Data

Bell, Samantha.
  Sports Medicine Doctor/Samantha Bell.
    pages cm.—(Cool STEAM careers)
  Summary: "Readers will learn what it takes to succeed as a sports medicine doctor. The book also explains the necessary educational steps, useful character traits, potential hazards, and daily job tasks related to this career. Sidebars include thought-provoking trivia. Questions in the backmatter ask for text-dependent analysis. Photos, a glossary, and additional resources are included"—Provided by publisher.
  Audience: Ages 8–12.
  Audience: Grades 4–6.
  Includes bibliographical references and index.
  ISBN 978-1-63362-564-8 (hardcover)—ISBN 978-1-63362-744-4 (pdf)—ISBN 978-1-63362-654-6 (pbk.)—
ISBN 978-1-63362-834-2 (ebook)
  1. Sports physicians—Juvenile literature. 2. Sports medicine—Vocational guidance—Juvenile literature. I. Title.
II. Series: 21st century skills library. Cool STEAM careers.

  RC1210.B35 2016
  617.1'027023—dc23
                              2015005365

Cherry Lake Publishing would like to acknowledge the work of
the Partnership for 21st Century Skills. Please visit www.p21.org
for more information.

Printed in the United States of America
Corporate Graphics

ABOUT THE AUTHOR

Samantha Bell is a children's writer and illustrator living in South Carolina with her husband, four children, and lots of animals.

TABLE OF CONTENTS

STEAM is the acronym for Science, Technology, Engineering, Arts, and Mathematics. In this book, you will read about how each of these study areas is connected to a career in sports medicine.

READY TO HELP

Usually, Sarah enjoyed watching her brother, Eric, and his college team play football. But this time, Eric's best friend, Robert, was hit hard and knocked to the ground. He didn't get up, and Sarah saw him grab his shoulder in great pain. The team's sports medicine doctor ran onto the field.

Sarah watched as Robert was helped off the field and into an ambulance. "Will he be all right?" she asked her dad.

"It looks like Robert hurt his shoulder," her dad replied. "He will have to have several tests, x-rays, and possibly other scans done. Then the doctors will know how to help him."

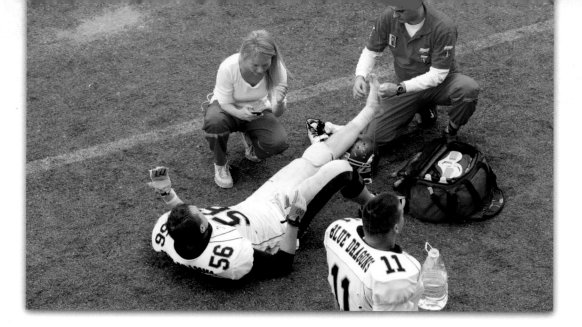

Sports medicine doctors are often present on the sidelines, ready to help if a player gets hurt.

"Will he be able to play again?" Sarah asked, her concern growing.

"It could take a while," her dad said. "He might have a long time of **rehabilitation**. He may have to wait until next season to rejoin the team."

For most sports doctors, working with a team is only one part of their **medical practice**. Sometimes they work with sports teams, or their patients may include dancers or marathoners. They have a special interest in treating injuries to muscles, bones, and joints. They

*Doctors' knowledge of the human skeleton
has improved a lot in the last few hundred years.*

treat anyone who is physically active.

Many historians trace the beginning of sports medicine to the ancient Greeks, over 2,000 years ago. These early doctors used similar supplies to those used today. **Splints** kept injured joints from moving. Casts helped broken bones to heal. Stitches closed wounds.

Scientists and doctors continued to learn about the human body. In 1569, the Italian doctor Geronimo Mercuriali (1530–1606) wrote the first illustrated book on sports medicine.

During the 1800s, some U.S. colleges started programs in gymnastics and football. Doctors were hired to care for the athletes' injuries. In 1928, doctors from several countries met in Switzerland and founded the International Assembly on Sports Medicine.

Today, more and more people of all ages are exercising and taking part in sports. When they are injured, many are treated by a sports doctor. Sports doctors work to help patients prevent injuries, improve performance, and increase overall health.

THINK ABOUT ART

Art has been a part of the study of medicine for hundreds of years. Leonardo da Vinci (1452–1519), the Italian artist and scientist, studied and made sketches of how people moved. Geronimo Mercuriali's book on sports medicine had pictures of people climbing ropes and using medicine balls for exercise. Even today, many sports medicine books and journals are illustrated with drawings.

BECOMING A SPORTS DOCTOR

All doctors choose an area of medicine to specialize in. Many of them choose family practice, pediatrics, orthopedics, or emergency medicine. Some of these specialists then become even more specialized. They become sports doctors.

Sports doctors must have good "people skills" because they work with many kinds of people. They have to get their ideas across to the athletes they treat. They must also talk to the athlete's family and coach. If the athlete is on a team, the sports doctor might also

A sports medicine doctor has to make her patients feel comfortable.

communicate with the athlete's teammates. Empathy, compassion, and good communications skills are important. If the doctor once had a sports injury, that might help him or her better understand what the patients are going through.

If becoming a sports medicine doctor interests you, you should take as many high school science classes as possible, such as biology and chemistry. You could also work as an assistant to the school's sports doctor or athletic trainer.

Chemistry classes are helpful for future sports medicine doctors.

To become a sports medicine doctor, you must go to college. Many students enroll in a premedical program. In this program, they take classes such as anatomy, biology, chemistry, **physiology**, and mathematics. During the third year of college, anyone planning on being a doctor must take the Medical College Admission Test (MCAT). Only students with high college grades and high MCAT scores are admitted to medical school.

Medical school is a four-year program. During the first two years, students spend most of their time in the classroom. The last two years, they are guided by doctors as they work with patients in hospitals. At the end of the four years, many medical students receive the doctor of medicine degree (MD), while some who took a different path become osteopathic doctors (DO). But both types still have several more years of training to complete before they can become practicing physicians.

After medical school, some doctors enter a multiyear residency program, where they learn a specialty, such as

A sports medicine doctor needs to know how to identify what type of injury the athlete has, and then treat it.

pediatrics or orthopedics. Most doctors interested in sports medicine enter a family medicine residency. When they finish the program, they take tests to become **certified** to practice their specialty.

The final step in becoming a sports doctor is enrolling in a sports medicine fellowship program. These specialized programs train doctors to prevent, identify, and treat sports injuries. Doctors spend one or two years in this program.

THINK ABOUT SCIENCE

People who become sports doctors should love learning about science. They must take science courses in high school, college, and medical school. But the learning doesn't stop there. Sports doctors must stay up to date on advancements in science and medicine. They must keep learning as our understanding of the human body continues to grow.

ON THE JOB

The main work of sports doctors is to prevent and to treat injuries in athletes and active individuals. To prevent injuries, sports doctors usually perform a physical examination before an athlete takes part in a sport. The exam might show that an athlete is overweight or underweight. Maybe an athlete should build up strength in a muscle. Maybe muscle tightness is preventing a joint from moving as much as it could. The sports doctor then suggests stretches for the athlete to practice, a change in diet, or a rest from certain

A sports medicine doctor will check a patient's physical progress.

activities (such as lifting heavy boxes). After this exam, the sports doctor will follow up with the athlete to make sure he or she is feeling stronger and not in much pain. If the athlete follows the directions, they're less likely to get injured when they begin their sports season.

Sports doctors also identify and treat athletes' injuries. Most of these injuries involve broken bones, **strained** muscles, **sprained ligaments**, and damaged joints. First, the doctor determines the amount of damage. This can sometimes be done by looking at or

An athlete may have to practice certain exercises in rehabilitation.

feeling the injury. Sometimes an ice pack, heat pack, or some anti-inflammatory medication is all that is needed. Sometimes a sports doctor orders an x-ray or an MRI of the painful joint to see how badly it is injured.

Most sports doctors work in a sports medicine clinic or hospital. This is where they perform physical examinations. This is also where they check patients' progress with rehabilitation exercises. They may work with several other sports doctors. These doctors share equipment and other staff, such as physical therapists, nurses, and record keepers.

Many sports doctors work with athletes on high school or college teams. These doctors give team members physical examinations. Sometimes athletes are injured during a game. The sports doctor decides if the injured player should be taken out of the game, and when—or if—they can be put back in.

This tennis player was injured during a match.

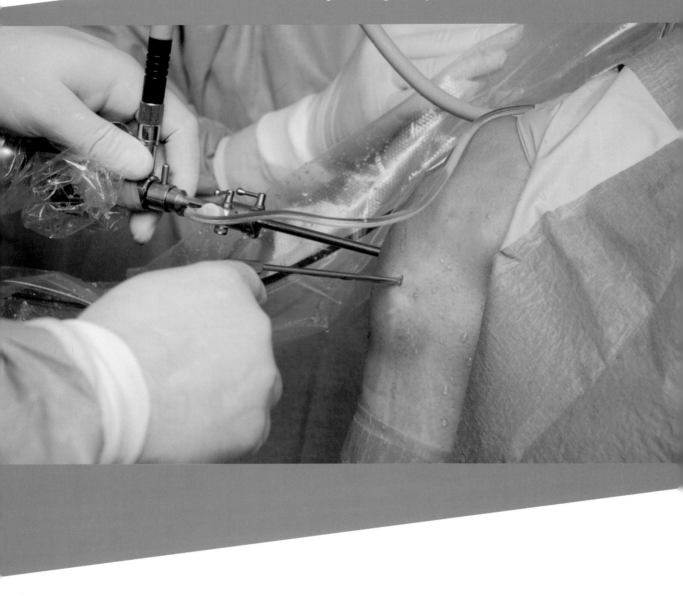

Some orthopedic surgeons specialize in knee surgery.

Some doctors train a little differently and become surgeons who specialize in bones and muscles, or **orthopedic surgeons**. They often work closely with sports doctors to treat patients. Surgeries take place in hospital operating rooms. Joints, muscles, and tendons take a long time to fully heal, but once the patient has recovered enough, the sports doctor may prescribe him or her a rehabilitation program. Rehabilitation programs start after an injury has healed. Exercise is usually a large part of these programs. They help athletes rebuild strength and regain flexibility.

THINK ABOUT ENGINEERING

In a way, sports doctors are like engineers—constantly looking for new ways to solve problems. Every year, better, safer, and stronger sports equipment is designed, such as the Rawlings S100 Pro Comp, a new batting helmet that baseball players wear. It protects their heads from wild pitches, making them a lot less likely to get concussions.

BENEFITS AND DISADVANTAGES

As a sports doctor, you can help athletes stay safe, perform their best in sporting events, and recover if an injury occurs. You can provide support and aid to dancers and other performers. You can also help those who just want to be more physically active. All of this can be very rewarding.

Unlike many athletes, sports doctors don't generally retire in their thirties. While athletes' careers usually end when they grow older and slow down, doctors can continue to practice medicine throughout their lives.

Alexis Sánchez, an FC Barcelona player, was injured in a match in 2012.

A few sports doctors work with professional sports teams. Some work with individual athletes such as figure skaters or golfers. They travel all over the world with the athletes to games and competitions.

While there are many benefits, the career has some disadvantages, too. Becoming a sports doctor takes years of expensive, stressful education and training. It also takes many years of experience before sports doctors are hired to work with professional athletes. These doctors are usually some of the best-known people in their field.

Swiss skier Dominique Gisin broke her leg in January 2015. Here, she races in France in 2010.

Dr. James Andrews has been practicing medicine for over 40 years. He specializes in knees, elbows, and shoulders. His lengthy patient list includes the football players Robert Griffin III and Peyton Manning, and the skier Lindsey Vonn. He's also treated so many baseball players that in 2014, Topps put him on his own baseball card! He says the key to injury prevention is that young players should take a couple months off a year to rest and recover. When middle school athletes train year-round the way professional athletes do, their bodies can't handle the stress, and they're more likely to need surgery later on.

THINK ABOUT MATH

Like others in medical professions, sports doctors must be able to use math. They need math to analyze data from tests and calculate dosages of medicine. They use it to determine the range of movement in injured and treated areas. As technology continues to advance, doctors may need to understand even more math to apply new techniques correctly.

Today and Tomorrow

Millions upon millions of people across the world participate in sports. Students join school teams. Some adults join their company's softball team. Others start running or using weights. Senior citizens get together to play golf. Sports injuries can happen to any of these people, but sports doctors are there to help all of them.

Sports doctors should expect many changes in their career. The number of jobs will continue to increase because so many people are becoming physically active. More people will need sports doctors to help them avoid and treat injuries. Sports teams at all levels are expected to hire more sports doctors. More high schools will start to hire sports doctors, at least on a part-time basis. Some experts believe that owners of professional athletic teams will add more specialists to their staffs. These doctors will specialize in injuries to certain parts of the body.

Many high school and college teams have hired their own sports medicine doctors.

A doctor needs to know the best exercises to recommend for each patient.

Doctors and scientists continue to develop new tools and equipment for treating injuries. They also develop more effective exercises for rehabilitation. All of these improvements help people return to their sport or activity faster after an injury. To help their patients, sports doctors will have to keep up with these changes. They will have to become experts at using these new treatments, tools, and equipment.

THINK ABOUT TECHNOLOGY

Medical equipment is constantly being improved as technology changes. Much of the new equipment for surgery and rehabilitation uses computers. Robotic surgery, which is still fairly new, requires doctors to use remote-controlled instruments. The robots make very small incisions, which shortens the patients' recovery times and gets them back on the field sooner. Sports medicine doctors must stay up to date on these advancements in technology to help their patients in the best ways possible.

Because of their specialized skills, sports doctors can earn a large salary. If they practice in clinics, their average annual salary could be $200,000. Those who are also orthopedic surgeons could earn more than $375,000 a year. Sports doctors who work for professional sports teams can earn $1 million or more a year.

Do you like to help people get and stay physically active? Do you like working with people in a variety of different situations? Do you get good grades in science classes? If you answered yes to these questions, then being a sports medicine doctor may be a good career choice for you.

A career in sports medicine can be very fulfilling.

THINK ABOUT IT

Ask an athlete you know if he or she has ever had an injury. Did he or she have to see a sports medicine doctor? What was his or her recovery like?

Go online and find the current roster for your favorite professional sports team. How many players are currently injured? Are any of their injuries similar? Are there any who have been injured before but are playing again? What advice do you think a sports medicine doctor would give them?

Sometimes, athletes are so badly injured that they have to take the rest of the season off, or even stop competing forever. Even if the doctor gives the best treatment possible, it might not be enough. How do you think a sports medicine doctor would tell an athlete that bad news? What would be some things he or she has to think about?

LEARN MORE

FURTHER READING

Devantier, Alecia T., and Carol A. Turkington. *Extraordinary Jobs in Sports*. New York: Ferguson Publishing, 2007.

Ferguson's Careers in Focus: Physicians. New York: Ferguson Publishing, 2006.

What Can I Do Now?—Sport. New York: Ferguson Publishing, 2007.

WEB SITES

American Medical Society for Sports Medicine: What Is a Sports Medicine Physician?
www.amssm.org/BrochureImages/WhatisaSportsMe-1.pdf
Print out a brochure that explains what a sports medicine physician does.

Minority Nurse: Playing Games
www.minoritynurse.com/article/playing-games
Read an article about sports medicine careers.

Next Impulse Sports: Here's the 7 Greatest Injury Comebacks in Sports History
http://nextimpulsesports.com/2014/08/04/heres-7-greatest-injury-comebacks-sports
-history
Check out this slideshow of athletes who have made amazing recoveries.

GLOSSARY

certified (SUR-tuh-fyed) officially approved to be able to do a job, usually after passing a test

ligaments (LIG-uh-muhntz) thick bands of tissue that connect one bone to another bone

medical practice (MED-uh-kuhl PRAK-tuhss) the business or work of a doctor

orthopedic surgeons (or-thuh-PEE-dik SUR-juhnz) doctors who perform operations to repair injuries to muscles, bones, and joints

physiology (fih-zee-AH-luh-jee) the study of the activities of the body's tissues and cells

rehabilitation (ree-huh-bi-luh-TAY-shuhn) special activities, exercises, or other programs that return an athlete to normal health after an injury

splints (SPLINTZ) pieces of wood, plastic, or metal used to prevent movement of a joint or to support an injured arm or leg

sprained (SPRAYND) stretched or tore a ligament

strained (STRAYND) stretched or tore a muscle or tendon

INDEX

[21ST CENTURY SKILLS LIBRARY]